Perpend Through Self Dignity

Kitty-ffion Vickerton-levis

BookLeaf Publishing

Presentation by *BookLeaf Publishing*

Web: www.bookleafpub.com

E-mail: info@bookleafpub.com

ISBN: 9789358369830

First edition 2023

*To my husband and to Georgia for without
either I could not wander on.*

Wander

I wander forward
Without true direction
I wander forward

I wander forward
With no path or map or even guide
I wander forward

I wander forward
Through fear and memory , paused briefly by
flashback yet still
I wander forward

I wander forward
Not ever knowing if safety or Dignity, if
freeness or faith are even tangible destinations
and even so
I wander forward

I wander forward
Why?

I wander forward
Behind is known.
I wander forward

I wander forward
For hope might just be on that next turn.
I wander forward
When dark is all there is,there must be light
ahead
I wander forward
In aimless search but that's okay
I wander forward
If all I have is the energy to breathe and continue
ahead that's all I need
I wander forward

I wander forward
I will get through this
I wander forward

You will get through this
Please
Wander forward

Sky water

Rain rain go away !

No wait I changed my mind.
Rain you are exactly what I need.

Perfect water falling , never a surprising texture
or noise or smell
As rain your character never truly changes.

I know your feeling rain and its safe and I can
predict my reaction to you
So stay.

Wash onto me and fill me with a constant.
Cold and chilling even on hot days,
Refreshing and setting and known.

Sky water falls of pretty droplets ,no matter the
volume
Soon to hit a target and replenish them.

Yes your mood wanders from gentle to
 Fury but for me your moods are vast but never
dangerous.
your presence is reassuring so

Rain stay.

No matter how heavy or gentle
you hug me rain just the way I need

When the sun is so adored,know I find my safe
in you sky water.

Rain rain go and pour

Reset. Replenish.Restore

Easy to give but hard to get

GET HELP
They say from all angles.
Talk to your GP or network or Charity
You can't just sit and simmer
Letting your internal light get dimmer.

GET HELP
They say with voices loud and proud
Like I haven't thought of this before
Truth is ,I've asked until voice sore
ashamed to admit dropped to my knees and
begged.

GET HELP
Say the doctors but not from us
You are to complicated for our criteria.
Also say the charity, to high is my hysteria,
So no help is coming from left or right.

GET HELP
Not very easy for the lost causes
The turned away at every angle
Holding the rope and tempted to strangle
But not ready to loose all hope

GET HELP
From inside yourself
Time ticking hobbies I tried next
Arts , crafts, sports, written text
Anything to pass an hour

GET HELP
Okay I will and I'll keep trying
I'll keep looking I'm not sure where
This inadequate support system isn't fare
So give me time

GET HELP
Try what support have you got?
Can I do anything for you?
Get help isn't simple I wish you knew.
Those words aren't helpful.

Fastnet

In the wind and waves of fierce height
Where blackness reaches maps edge
Upon jagged rock mound upright
She stands tall , unwavering with her light

Wiery souls sail lost not certain
Of earth that's safe for landing
Ground to keep them from their burden
She stays high and guiding as the storms do
worsen.

Pass by her with careful wide birth
As she warns you of unseen danger around
Yet the lady knows of all lost souls worth
So stands continual until the safe dawns rebirth

In calmer days her grand silhouette
Stands dark compared to sun
Her power ,her support too easily forgot
When you are lost she'll extend her grace to all
without a sweat.

Built to weather every strengthened storm
From the rough hands of man
The miracle of rescue she does perform

Through churning weather reform

So look up to our dear Fasnet
Even though she's weather witherd
Continual it may be, admire her survived threat
For her story is long in history set.

In the wind and waves of fierce height
Where blackness reaches maps edge
Upon jagged rock mound upright
You stand tall , unwavering with your light

Take your storms and learn to guide
Those less fortunate with no knowledge
How to,from horror and memory hide
Stretch out your light and keep them safe aside.

All the little noises

The world is incredibly loud.

Even in the "quite" spaces noise still fills the air.

Monitors buzzing, aircon wers , keyboard insesent tapping , then add the out of sync breathing of each individual in there as well as their personal muttering.

Throw in the multitude of one way conversations over teams , relevant to you and completely irrelevant. Did you know plug sockets sing a little electric sound? It's really annoying.

Let's add in notification noises the little creeks of the chairs being moved that odd flicker of the ceiling lights and all these little noises are now a ball of large unstoppable sound I am holding my breathe to calm my nerve because you can't hear all this but I can and I am about to shout to be heard when all I need to do is speak calmly and if I don't inhale again soon I will snap

Inhale.exhale.repeat

Splay hands flat on your desk ,heels to the floor
and breathe.
When your able chin up , sit with your back up
to the backrest and relax that tongue from the
top of your mouth.
Inhale.exhale.repeat

This is just noise. It can't hurt you
I agree your ears are hurting and your brains
going fuzzy but physically your fine.
So breathe and keep breathing.

Find the corners of the room.
At the ceiling and at the floor.
Find the windows or the main walls.
Feel your feet against the floor.

The room is incredibly loud.
So darling you be incredibly proud.
That you can be here and part of it
Learning and growing to keep going.

All the little noises build to bigger sound
So plant your feet firmly , keep them safely to
the ground.

It has to go somewhere

AAAAAAAAAAAAAAAAAAAAAAAAAAAAAA
AH
AAAAAAAAAAAAAAAAAAAAAAAAAAAAH
H
AAAAAAAAAAAAAAAAAAAAAAAAAAHH
AAAAAAAAAAAAAAAAAAAAHHHHH

AAAAAAAAAAAAAAAAAAAAAH
AAAAAAAAAAAAAAAAAHHH
AAAAAAAAAAAAAAAHHHH
AAaaaaaaaaaaaaaaaaaah
aaaaaaaaaaaaaaaaaah
aaaaaaaaaaaaaaaah
aaaaaaaaaaaaah
aaaaaaaaah
aaaaaaah
aaaaah
aah
aw

Bit better now, all that's out.

Georgia

There's a kind of friendship forged in pain
The dark humour laughter that keeps you sane.
That friend who met you in the shadows,
Dragged you back from deep to shallows,
That one who knows your every secret
Comforts you from your constant regret.

The friend who knows you'd rather not be here,
They feel the same and share in fear.
The one you can hug when no one else feels
right
The one you help ground when they wish to take
flight.

That friend who laughs with you when every
one else worries
The one you stand tall with when the trauma
brain scurries.
The one you can call and talk to for hours
Over nothing at all or to let out tear showers.

And you give to them what they give to you
And their importance you wish they knew.
When you have only 10% they'll give 90,
When they only have 10 , you'll stand mighty.

Taking in turns to keep the demons at bay
And silencing the negative voices that say
All of the things you believe about yourself
They'll lift you up , keep an eye on your health.

This friend is golden and perfect and pure
Even though they are as broken as you, for sure.
You found each other abandoned and alone
Just as your souls where turning stone.

Over time, you've helped each other to feel
Piece by piece supporting to heal.
So many years on ,your still friends at large
Helping each other learning to recharge.

Holding space for you both to grieve
For a life you knew you couldn't perceive,
The one without such suffocating pain
The one where you where both normal and sane

On this timeline our paths crossed
all through our lives there's been high cost
But I'd spend it again if it meant
In my direction you'd be sent.

What is a hero?

Some heroes wear capes
Mostly, those heroes who don't actually exist
Who appear on paper as lycra clad gods
And tear up cities somehow in the name of good
to protect mear humans from all odds.

Actual heroes wear normal clothes
The kind you get in everyday shops
They blend so well you'd hardly know their
there.
But when they help the pain and sorrow stops.

Real heroes don't magically resolve unfixable
problems
But they certainly won't leave you all alone to
face them.
They stand ,holding your hand providing small
shines of a positive gem.

Our hereos are quite common
The steps who came along and filled broken
hearts.
Or the arms that grabbed on,
not letting go of broken parts.

Maybe stop searching for the extra
Because we start to miss the special.
The quite souls who help others
who listen, who learn
And really aren't judgemental.

I've started to see heroes
Nearly almost everyday
Sometimes silently supporting
Maybe even give it a go ?
I can imagine it's quite rewarding

How?

There are parts of me
That I've shared without wanting to.
Pieces of my skin touched, over and over
without my consent.

Kissed but not with love and care
Caressed in ways dark and unimaginable
And yet someone imagined it because they did it
and where capable.
This person carried on and on
While I pleaded and whimpered only to learn to
fall silent.

Sometimes this process was violent
And I had the courage which I now, view
through trauma glasses, as stupidity
To fight back!
So the injuries would be enough to mark but not
mame ,
My attacker was not stupid and I knew his name.

He knew every gaslighting trick in the book
I don't know the person I was before him.
I can't reach her.

I only know who I was during and who I suffer
with now after.

They tell you to hold onto hope of the future.
I was told over and over "no one will help you
or belive you because I'll tell them your crazy!"
And I held on to hope of a future
Where the world would prove him wrong.

Once again I was wrong.
Wrong to have hope of a world where victims
with mental health diagnosis
Are treated as valid equals.
One where we get happy endings or
Fare starts for new sequels.

I learned that in a court you'll have it held
against you, its where they use your diagnosis
,which they do not understand
To discredit your character
Paint you as a useless witness
And claim the upper hand.
So in the story of your own attack
You're memory and evidence becomes futile
While the jury thinks your truth is hostile.

So even though now with a new diagnosis of
severe PTSD
No one with the power to stop him

Will listen to what happened to me.
No ones coming to save me or provide justice
for this fear
He moves on with a clean bill to hurt again
While I struggle every day in every year.

I thought the hardest words I ever heard
Was 'Not guilty'
The hardest words I ever heard was that I don't
have EUPD , the label held against me to paint
the picture of an unstable liar.
The hardest pill to swallow was you were
misdiagnosed. You are autistic.

I am autistic.
Amongst life long issues with nearly everything
in the world.
I am vulnerable to safe relationships because I
don't read emotion well or understand social
expectations.
So I carried on thinking it was normal hardship,
I learn every day new ways how it was abuse.
I recall through flashback and trauma how he
tightened the metaphorical knoose.

The world didn't understand me before the
PTSD was added ontop
It definitely doesn't understand me now.

So I pick up pieces and try to bring my best self
to the daily table
But all I can do is stand back and think
How. How....how ?

Two tiny faces

I have two tiny faces.
Tiny faces who look up to me to guide,
Lead the way in life
Journey through the shadows for them

My role is to help them gently
to find who they are in this world
To play and support and grow
to keep them safe and in the know.

I am their hope and their light
I try to be their calm when they bubble over
I need to be their solice in storm
To keep them balanced in the norm.

I have two tiny faces
Whome I am supposed to save
And yet they saved me
I had no clue where to go
Having them has grounded me.

I have two tiny faces
They give me reason
They give me hope
They're beacons of light in my storms.

Imposter syndrome

Leave a little room to grow
I say time and time again.
Hoping that soon the void of imposter syndrome
with fall into the background,
I will acknowledge I found my feet ,feel like I'm
flying like I belong .like I'm a part of this.
Wake up and fit right into a team,
Provide something useful to the table.

For now it feels like I bring nothing.
I tag along like a painful burden
Unable to keep up or provide ,
Unable to reach that sky
These feelings do not subside
Measured against progress I fall far behind.
Whilst those around take repeated 2 steps
forward , I take 2 and 1 back.
Permanently lacking.

2 steps forward and 1 step back.

2 steps forward and 1 step back.

That's still 1 step further then I was yesterday.
That's a sign I'm getting somewhere,

That's a signal to have some care
In a positive way toward my goal
I'm not lacking I'm getting there !

It takes me longer I know
And though I feel it I'm not an imposter
I am just as deserving and this is the emotion I
need to Foster,
My brain is flawed and scared and broken
And here I am still 2 steps forward 1 step back
and yes, yes that's still 1 forward.
A single step a day is still a point of pride
When walking isn't easy and PTSD affects every
stride.
Throw in the autism and that I don't fit in
anywhere , ever
1 step a day is getting somewhere -not as fast
but its still clever.

I make progress by purely choosing
One.more.day
That's the progress I make add that I'm finally
trying for a career
No wonder I feel lost like I shouldn't be here.
While most younger folk talked about careers
and goals and learning.
What their future would hold what they'd be
earning,

I fought desperately hard to simply never see
another sunrise.
I couldn't see a world where me being older then
18 would arise.

Now at 26 with yet more trauma added to the
plate,
I'm learning to work and parent and emotionally
regulate.
I'm joining the rat race late.
I don't know how to fit here
But one day I know it will become clear.

For now I'll take my 2 steps forward and 1 step
back because its further then I was yesterday.

Not as far as the rest of my peers but still not
stagnant.

Not as clear as my team in direction
But I need to adjust my expectation.

I deserve to be here
You deserve to be here
We all deserve to just be here.

Night

There is something calming upon the night,
The gentle darkness filled with hidden life.
The shadows of creatures all roaming their
kingdoms,
Unaware that to most the night is terror,
Symbolism of the end or unknown
But this is their comfort and happy home.

The silent ones who've learned to navigate their
space leaving no trace ,
Of where they've come from before or where
they will head to.
Take solice in that calm and quite world
Of gentle dark and life that has adapted to thrive
without light
Life that never gave up , who sees
The start not end marked by night.

Listen to the subtle sounds
Of moth wings and creature paws padding
against cool mossy floors.
Floors you can't see but know they are there
through feeling.
Floors that catch you from the thought of ever
falling.

The dark night is a friend
More approachable through the brilliance of the
stars it offers.
Glimmers and glitters of far off perfection
That kick start positive inward reflection.
Take time to sit with the night
Enjoy its hospitality as it takes your chaos and
stims it down to manageable equilibrium of
emotion.

Easy days

It's a strange kind of day
When the troubles melt away,
The cup of tea hits the right spot
The morning is nice , no stressful plot.

The triggers haven't knocked on the door
You don't need to feel for the floor,
The breeze is cool and right
There is no need to mentally fight.

It's a calm kind of 24 hours
One to pause and take in the flowers.
Ends in an eve with blankets to snuggle
A super rare day without any struggle.

There will be these days
In-between the not fun maze
Hold onto these breaks of rest
The days that provide no test.

The ones where you can breath and pause
The ones with no direction or cause
The ones to just stop and be
Of the chaos a little bit free.

Hot chocolate

27

Hot chocolate has so many great things
About it.

On chesty days it helps me breathe.
On dark days it helps me believe.
On stress days it helps me relieve.
On sad days it helps me grieve.
On forward days it helps me achieve.
On needing days it helps me retrieve.
On confused days it helps me conceive.
On long days it closes the eve.
On boring days it helps make believe
Dark memories it helps me leave.

Hot chocolate has so many great things About it
!

What's your drink of choice ?

Painting nails.

I love to do my nails !

Every colour of the rainbow ,
A different shape and style every time.
Pretty stamps or glitter streaks.

I love to do my nails!

Taking time to be with myself
Finding small joys to attach to me
And creating tiny little pieces of art

I love to do my nails!

To focus so hard on small details
That my brain can't think of anything else
Just painting 10 individual canvases

I love to paint my nails!

A little enjoyment within your day
Can really make the difference.
So find away to go forward
Have an activity to take your mind away.

I love to paint my nails.

Kit

Loud and lary and bright.
I'll force confidence with all my might,
I'll step into a room like I own it
Speak loudly and do my bit.

Inside away from eyes I tremble
Words are lost as I try to assemble
Them into clear sentences to share
And make my point clear and fare.

But they will not see this
To them a pause won't go a miss,
So take a breath and and fake it all the way
cause I have something important to say.

I am not woman. Not not anymore
I left her behind shut behind a door
Of unwanted memories and history
I am gender fluid . THIS is me.

They/them are perfect pronouns
Kit is the name I pronounce
I know who they are in the mirror
For my reflection I do not whimper.

I found how to love me ,know who I am!
So your opinion , I don't give a damn
Because literally I've stood over the bridge
Wanting to die I've tried to manage.

Through out my 26 years of history
I've attempted 41 times to finish me
Thankfully the thing I'm bad at is suicide
I'm grateful I failed everytime I tried.

Look at me now, look where I came
Far from girl who could only shoulder blame
For not being happy who hurt over and over
Unaware of the true self left to discover.

So again I say as loud as I can
My name is Kit , they/them I am.
I've survived the hardest going test
The journey of the self-discovery quest.

So now you know a small snapshot
All I ask is try not to use something I'm not.
I know it's not easy , I did this challenge too
Trying is all I ask you to do.

Neither here nor there

There's a difference outside of the home
Where you feel lost and somewhat alone
The safety blanket torn away
The fears of the strange here to stay.

That not knowing what trigger comes next
The reality that the outside is so complex
Suddenly no control of the noise level
Feeling like the world is the devil

A chance of being bumped into
Physical touch you can't get through
The tight grasp panic starts to set in
You wish you where tiny unseen thin

The outside has faces that you don't know
That mirror your abuser even though
They are not him but flashbacks take hold
Even when your story is untold.

Voices blend into unsafe spaces
Feeling like there's no calm places
To exist and be outside of your house
No ones safe , not even your spouse.

Trauma repeats itself in wierd ways
With symptoms taking up your days
Wiping your memory of most of the fun
Making contact feel like a gun

I didn't know it literally changes your brain
Your cognitive map will never be the same
And yet the world expects you to fit right in
Not showing signs that you hate your skin

There's another important aspect to trauma
You kind find solice amongst the fauna
Find your place back within nature
For they will help your soul to nurture

Walk and breathe in the crisp air
Find your piece in the quite and fair
Meditate outside and take in the flowers
Pass by the time , pass by the hours.

Trauma will takeover so much of you
So win it back by finding some new
Places to spend time and reflection
Making pathways for future connection

Being free

I never chose to be queer,
I woke up and just knew I was here.
The older I get the more I learn
That I was never once straight in my life.

Look let's be real I was to young to know what
love was, but boy did I like to show
Every possible piece of clothing I had
I would parade as male or female or both at
once.

not care one ounce about the world around
To sing and dance and make a sound
And be utterly free because as I a kid no one
seems to mind as much because its a 'phase'.

But you hit puberty, there's no clean slate
And it doesn't seem to make you 'straight'
All of a sudden your amazing personality
matters and the people who loved you don't
anymore.

Rainbows are suddenly not pretty pictures
Their symbols of community structures

Now it raises eyebrows when you show the
world who you are and for the first time at about
7 or 8 you know to hate yourself.

7 or 8 is when I knew I was different
When I learned hiding me was convenient
Better to try to align as a pretty girl
Who had interest in handsome boys ,to plan to
bring home the new man of the house.

Ironically I have found love in a man
Who let's me be out and proud as I am
Who loves the light I can bring to world and the
joy that identifying correctly brings me and
doesn't care that I could be interested in man or
women and who ever is in-between.

The hardest part about the world I knew
Is knowing what boxing in a child can do
And now I have two, currently, sons
I have not 1 idea how to raise them safely and
correctly to authentically exist and be proud of
who ever they grow to be.

All I can do is show them that I don't fear
Being out and bright and proud and here
To work to bring safety and support to our
community where ever I can and voice what
others might not be able to.

I am pretty young and I can say still
The world has grown but its uphill
And there's always strides to continue forward
for inclusion and diversity, its getting there but
we can't stop this momentum.

We can make changes around us
To be ourselves and cause a fuss
At first as people start to get used to the knew
identities which have actually been around
forever, but only now are safe enough to show
themselves.

Be a listening ear if needed
Be kind
Be a shoulder to cry on
Be kind
Be an ally
Be kind
Be your authentic self who ever that person is.
Be kind
Be open
Be kind
Be honest
Be kind

Dear any one who may listen just be kind.

And together we can take that uphill walk
We can have the difficult talk
So that maybe in the future parents won't be
terrified on how to raise their children to know
they are loved no matter who they are or who
the love.

Okay

It's okay
To be struggling

It's okay
To broken

It's okay
To find it impossible

It's okay
To not know what tomorrow brings

It's okay
To have all the energy now but drained later

Its okay
To rest

It's okay
To sleep

It's okay
To eat

It's okay

To cry

It's okay
To feel everything and nothing

It's okay
Being you

Don't feel you are ever not worthy
It's okay because you are worthy

Sway

Grass sways in rhythm
Never staying still even
When the wind is gone

The end of this book

Books end all the time
Story's do not ,they go on being told
By new voices ;new faces, not growing old
So I like to hope that when my book does Finish,
My history ,my journey will not diminish
Instead somehow go on too inspire
Those that want to die find new fire
To carry on for one more sunrise
You don't know the futures suprise
Never in my wildest dreams did I think
I'd live with such a crippling trauma link
And yet at the same time have such days
That I still want to shout life's praise
This strange ever going adventure
I'm no longer a hopeless backbencher
Of life and of survival I am here !
And I'm okay with that. I have no fear
Of still breathing in the morning anymore
I adore my kids and husband to my core
I love who I am now becoming
And if I have no strength I'll be humming
To get me ready for tomorrow's song
Which I will enjoy all along.
Trauma doesn't seem to leave
It makes it really hard to breathe

But it doesn't stop my soul from singing
And life's pretty bell, I'll keep ringing
So this tiny snapshot book is ending
But I am not and I'm not spending
Life focused entirely on the bad
For most days I can just be glad
That I survived.

I survived.